Canada Post: Management failure to modernise mail systems

DM Ole Kiminta

Published by KMBros, 2024.

CANADA POST: MANAGEMENT FAILURE TO MODERNISE MAIL SYSTEMS

First edition. December 6, 2024.

ISBN: 979-8230970569

Written by DM Ole Kiminta.

Also by DM Ole Kiminta

How the Western Democracies failed the world
Supporting Refugees in their Homelands
Dissuading Global War Mongers:
Dissuading war mongers
La Libération Monétaire en Afrique
Canada Post: Management failure to modernise mail systems
Canada Post management failure to modernise mail systems
Canada Post: Management failure to modernise mail systems

Table of Contents

For Canada Post employees of:

Yesterday, Today

and Tomorrow

Your struggles continue

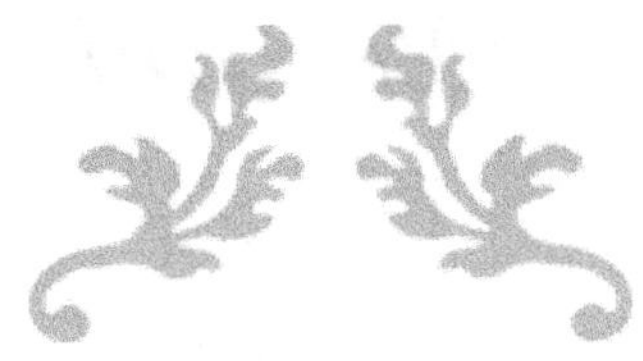

Canada Post management failure to modernise the mail systems

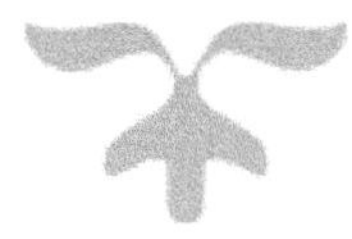

DM Ole Kiminta

The struggle continues (Gateway plant, Mississauga, Ontario Canada)

Historical Overview of Canada Post

There are those of us including most of the employees of this crown corporation who have watched from the sideline trying desperately to advise the management to hasten modernisation for a long time but have paradoxically been shrugged off by the management. The narrative on this short publication delves on the question of why those hired to update, watch, safeguard and keep up with the mail business competitiveness by concerting efforts to grab every possible opportunity to modernise the company did the *leissez faire* and skyved it off. Regrettably, the Management did not pay any particular attention to this humongous mistake but rather sat back and became spectators in spite of their high salary bracket and prodigious bonuses. The book also has more information that places Canada Post Corporation on the International Postal services (IPS) arena and what confronts mail and parcel systems in other countries worldwide.

Canada Post, established in 1867, has undergone significant transformations throughout its history. Initially created to facilitate communication across the vast expanse of Canada, the organisation became a critical service for connecting communities, particularly in remote and rural areas. As a Crown Corporation, it was designed to serve the public interest rather than to generate profit, which shaped its operational strategies and service offerings. Over the years, Canada Post expanded its services, including parcel delivery and logistics, adapting to the needs of a growing population and the evolving landscape of communication.

The late 20th century marked a pivotal moment for Canada Post, as technological advancements began to redefine the postal industry. With the advent of the internet and email, traditional mail volumes began to decline sharply. Canada Post faced mounting pressure to modernise its operations and enhance its service delivery to remain relevant. Despite these challenges, management struggled to implement effective strategies that would address the changing landscape. The reluctance to adopt innovative practices and invest in technology became a recurring theme in the organization's history, ultimately contributing to a perception of stagnation.

In the early 2000s, Canada Post introduced a series of strategic initiatives aimed at revitalising the organisation. These included efforts to improve customer service, streamline operations, and expand e-commerce capabilities. However, many of these initiatives were met with mixed results. Internal resistance to change, coupled with inadequate investment in modern technologies, hindered the effectiveness of these strategies. As competitors in the logistics and courier sectors began to embrace new technologies and customer-centric approaches, Canada Post struggled to keep pace, leading to further erosion of its market share.

The culmination of these challenges became evident in the late 2010s when Canada Post faced significant financial difficulties. Declining mail volumes, increased competition, and rising operational costs created a perfect storm that threatened the sustainability of the service. Management's failure to decisively modernise the organisation led to cuts in services and increased prices, prompting public outcry and dissatisfaction. The disconnect between management's strategic vision and the operational realities faced by the corporation underscored the need for a comprehensive reevaluation of Canada Post's approach to modernisation.

As Canada Post moves into the future, the lessons learned from its historical overview are crucial. The organisation must recognise the importance of adapting to the digital age, investing in technology, and fostering a culture of innovation. Acknowledging past management failures can serve as a foundation for rebuilding trust with the public and ensuring that Canada Post fulfills its mandate as a vital service provider. The ongoing challenge will be to balance the need for modernisation with the commitment to serve all Canadians, particularly those in underserved areas, as the industry continues to evolve.

The Role of Canada Post in Canadian Society

Canada Post has long served as a cornerstone of Canadian society, playing a crucial role in connecting communities across the vast expanse of the country. Established in 1867, the Crown corporation has evolved from a traditional postal service into a multifaceted entity that encompasses mail delivery, package shipping, and various financial services. Its extensive network reaches even the most remote areas, ensuring that Canadians have access to essential services. The role of Canada Post extends beyond mere logistics; it fosters social cohesion, economic growth, and accessibility, making it an integral part of daily life for millions.

In recent years, Canada Post has faced significant challenges in adapting to the rapid technological advancements that have transformed the way people communicate and conduct business. With the rise of digital communication, traditional mail volumes have declined, leading to a shift in the operational landscape. Canada Post's management has struggled to modernise its services in response to these changes, often falling behind private sector competitors who have embraced innovation and agile business practices. This failure to adapt has resulted in a loss of market share and a growing perception of Canada Post as an outdated institution.

The impact of Canada Post's management decisions extends beyond financial implications; it also affects the accessibility and reliability of postal services. Canadians in rural and remote areas rely heavily on Canada Post for essential deliveries, including healthcare products and vital correspondence. However, service disruptions and inconsistent delivery times have raised concerns about the corporation's ability to fulfill its mandate effectively. These operational shortcomings not only frustrate customers but also undermine trust in a service that is expected to be dependable and efficient.

Moreover, Canada Post plays a significant role in supporting small businesses and e-commerce. As online shopping continues to surge, the demand for reliable parcel delivery services has increased exponentially. Canada Post has the potential to leverage its extensive network to facilitate the growth of Canadian entrepreneurs, yet its failure to modernise has hindered its ability to compete effectively with private delivery services. By not investing adequately in technology and infrastructure, Canada Post risks alienating a crucial customer base that depends on timely and efficient delivery options.

The future of Canada Post hinges on its ability to address these management failures and embrace a more innovative approach. Reassessing its operational strategies, investing in new technologies, and prioritising customer service are essential steps toward reclaiming its position as a leader in the postal industry. By adapting to the changing landscape and meeting the needs of Canadians, Canada Post can reinforce its vital role in society and ensure its relevance in the years to come. The challenge lies in whether its management can pivot and recognise the importance of modernisation in safeguarding the corporation's legacy and service to the public.

Importance of Modernisation

The importance of modernisation in any organisation cannot be overstated, particularly for a Crown corporation like Canada Post. Modernisation is not merely about adopting new technologies; it involves a comprehensive approach to improving efficiency, enhancing customer service, and remaining relevant in a rapidly evolving marketplace. For Canada Post, the failure to modernise has resulted in significant operational challenges and a decline in public trust. As consumers increasingly demand faster and more reliable services, the inability to adapt has left Canada Post vulnerable to competition from private sector alternatives.

One of the key aspects of modernisation is the integration of technology into core operations. Canada Post has historically relied on traditional postal methods, which, while effective in the past, are no longer sufficient in today's digital age. The rise of e-commerce and digital communication has transformed the landscape of postal services. Competitors have embraced innovative solutions, such as automated sorting systems and real-time tracking, which have set new standards for efficiency and customer satisfaction. Canada Post's slow response to these changes has hindered its ability to compete effectively, leading to a loss of market share and relevance.

Moreover, modernisation is crucial for improving customer experience. In an era where consumers expect immediate gratification, delays and inefficiencies can lead to dissatisfaction and frustration. Canada Post's failure to modernise has resulted in outdated processes that do not meet the evolving needs of customers. For example, long wait times for parcel deliveries and inadequate tracking capabilities have driven customers to seek alternatives. By investing in modernisation initiatives, Canada Post could significantly enhance its service offerings, thereby restoring public confidence and loyalty.

The financial implications of modernisation are also significant. Investing in new technologies and processes can lead to substantial cost savings in the long run. Canada Post's reluctance to modernise has resulted in an increase in operational costs due to inefficiencies and the maintenance of outdated systems. By embracing modern practices, the organisation could streamline its operations, reduce overhead, and ultimately improve its bottom line. This financial stability is essential for fulfilling its mandate as a Crown corporation, which includes providing affordable and accessible postal services to all Canadians.

Finally, the importance of modernisation extends beyond operational efficiency and customer satisfaction; it is a matter of strategic survival. As the postal landscape continues to evolve, organisations that fail to adapt risk obsolescence. Canada Post's management must recognise that modernisation is not an option but a necessity. By committing to a comprehensive modernisation strategy, Canada Post can position itself as a leader in the postal sector, ensuring its relevance and sustainability in the face of future challenges. Embracing change is critical not only for the organisation’s growth but also for maintaining its role as a vital public service in Canada.

Chapter 2: The Management Structure

Overview of Canada Post Management

Canada Post, as a Crown corporation, has historically played a pivotal role in the communication and logistics landscape of Canada. It has evolved to meet the demands of a changing society, yet its management strategies have often come under scrutiny. The organisation has faced significant challenges in adapting to the rapid advancements in technology and shifts in consumer behavior, leading to questions about its ability to modernise effectively. The overview of Canada Post management highlights the key areas where decisions and practices have contributed to its struggles in navigating the complexities of the contemporary postal environment.

One critical aspect of Canada Post's management is its organisational structure, which has been criticised for being overly bureaucratic and resistant to change. The layers of hierarchy within the corporation can impede swift decision-making and limit the responsiveness needed in a fast-paced market. This structure has often resulted in delayed implementation of innovative practices, leaving Canada Post lagging behind competitors who have embraced more agile management approaches. The inability to streamline operations has also affected employee morale and productivity, creating an environment where adaptation to new technologies is met with hesitation.

Additionally, Canada Post's leadership has grappled with a lack of clear vision regarding its role in the digital age. While other postal services globally have embraced diversification and innovation, Canada Post has struggled to redefine its services beyond traditional mail delivery. This shortcoming has led to missed opportunities in expanding into e-commerce solutions and digital communications, both of which are critical for survival in an increasingly online world. Without a robust strategy to integrate these elements, Canada Post risks becoming obsolete, unable to offer relevant services to its customers.

As I write these few pages, Canada Post employees are on strike.(day 3). The management of Canada Post has also faced challenges in engaging with its workforce effectively. Employee relations have been marked by strikes and labor disputes, reflecting deeper issues of dissatisfaction and disconnection between management and staff. A lack of proactive communication and collaborative problem-solving has fostered an adversarial atmosphere, which stifles innovation and enthusiasm for modernisation initiatives. There are many low-ranked employees within the workforce in Canada Post who have come to work here after having been engineers, managers, lawyers, and much more yet, any one of them giving advice to any member of the management is scornfully brushed aside instead of trying to look at the suggestions. Addressing these internal dynamics is essential for fostering a culture that embraces change and seeks to improve service delivery.

In my opinion, the overview of Canada Post management reveals a complex interplay of structural, strategic, and interpersonal issues that have hindered the corporation's ability to modernise. As the postal landscape continues to evolve, Canada Post must confront these challenges head-on, reassessing its management practices and embracing a more dynamic approach to leadership. By doing so, it can better position itself to meet the demands of modern consumers and remain a vital component of Canada's communication infrastructure.

Governance and Accountability

Governance and accountability are critical components in the operation of any public institution, particularly for a Crown corporation like Canada Post. Governance refers to the frameworks, processes, and practices through which an organisation is directed and controlled, while accountability ensures that management is answerable to its stakeholders. In the case of Canada Post, the failure to establish robust governance structures and accountability mechanisms has significantly hindered its ability to modernise and adapt to the changing needs of its customers and the broader marketplace.

The governance framework of Canada Post has historically been characterised by a lack of clear strategic direction and insufficient oversight. The board of directors, responsible for ensuring that the corporation meets its responsibilities, has at times been composed of members with limited expertise in postal operations or modern business practices. This has led to decisions that do not adequately reflect the realities of the evolving postal landscape, where competition from private courier services and digital communication has intensified. Without a board that understands the nuances of the industry, Canada Post has struggled to formulate effective strategies aimed at innovation and customer service enhancement.

Accountability mechanisms within Canada Post have also been inadequate. While the corporation is required to report on its performance and strategic objectives, the metrics used to evaluate success often fail to address the core issues facing the organisation. For instance, performance indicators may focus on financial profitability rather than customer satisfaction or operational efficiency. This misalignment has resulted in a culture where short-term financial gains are prioritised over long-term sustainability and customer trust. Stakeholders, including the Canadian public, have been left in the dark regarding the true state of the organisation and its plans for modernisation.

Moreover, the lack of accountability extends to the management level, where leadership has often been insulated from the consequences of poor decision-making. In a rapidly changing environment, the ability to pivot and respond to external pressures is paramount. However, Canada Post's management has frequently been slow to react, hampered by bureaucratic inertia and a reluctance to embrace transformative changes. The absence of a clear accountability framework has allowed management to operate without sufficient scrutiny, leading to missed opportunities for innovation and modernisation.

To address these governance and accountability challenges, Canada Post must undertake a comprehensive revitalisation of its structures and practices. This includes the recruitment of board members with diverse expertise and a proven track record in modern business operations, as well as the establishment of more rigorous performance metrics that align with customer expectations. Furthermore, fostering a culture of accountability within management will be crucial in ensuring that decisions are made with a long-term vision in mind. By implementing these changes, Canada Post can better position itself to meet the demands of today's marketplace and regain the public's trust.

Decision-Making Processes

Decision-making processes within Canada Post have been a significant factor in the organisation's failure to modernise effectively. Historically, the management's approach to decision-making has been characterised by a top-down structure, where directives flowed from senior executives to lower levels without adequate input from frontline employees. This hierarchical model often led to decisions that did not reflect the realities of operations, customer needs, or the rapidly changing postal landscape. As a result, critical opportunities for innovation and adaptation were overlooked, contributing to the stagnation of the Crown Corporation.

One of the key issues in the decision-making process has been a lack of flexibility and responsiveness. In an age where technology and consumer expectations evolve quickly, Canada Post's management has often adhered to outdated practices and policies. This rigidity has impeded the organisation's ability to pivot in response to market demands or to embrace new technologies that could enhance service delivery. The failure to adopt a more agile decision-making framework has left the corporation vulnerable to competition from both traditional postal services and emerging delivery platforms.

Moreover, insufficient stakeholder engagement has been another critical shortfall. Effective decision-making should involve collaboration and consultation with various stakeholders, including employees, customers, and community partners. However, Canada Post's management has frequently made unilateral decisions without soliciting feedback or insights from those directly impacted. This disconnect has not only led to poor morale among employees but also to a misalignment between the services offered and the actual needs of the public. A more inclusive approach could have fostered innovation and better service delivery.

Additionally, the reliance on outdated data and metrics has hindered informed decision-making. Canada Post's management has often depended on historical performance indicators that do not accurately capture current trends or future projections. This reliance on obsolete data has resulted in strategic missteps and missed opportunities for growth. By failing to adopt modern analytical tools and metrics that reflect the current market environment, Canada Post has struggled to make decisions that align with contemporary consumer behaviors and expectations.

In conclusion, the decision-making processes at Canada Post have played a crucial role in its inability to modernise. The combination of a rigid hierarchical structure, lack of stakeholder engagement, reliance on outdated practices, and poor data utilisation has collectively stifled innovation and responsiveness. For Canada Post to regain its footing and effectively navigate the complexities of the modern postal landscape, it must critically reassess and reform its decision-making processes to foster agility, inclusivity, and data-driven strategies. Only then can it hope to meet the challenges posed by a rapidly changing environment and better serve the Canadian public.

Chapter 3: Early Signs of Trouble

Declining Mail Volumes

The decline in mail volumes has been a significant challenge for Canada Post, reflecting a broader trend observed globally in postal services. As digital communication technologies have advanced, traditional mail has experienced a sharp downturn. Canadians are increasingly opting for instant messaging, email, and social media platforms instead of relying on physical mail. This shift not only impacts the volume of mail processed but also raises questions about the sustainability of Canada Post's traditional business model, which has long relied on a steady flow of letters and parcels.

As the volume of mail declines, Canada Post has struggled to adapt its operations to this new reality. The organisation has been slow to implement modern solutions that could help streamline processes and reduce costs. While other postal services around the world have embraced technology and innovation, Canada Post has often lagged behind. This lack of responsiveness to changing consumer behaviors has led to inefficiencies and increased operational expenses, ultimately affecting the corporation's financial health and service delivery.

The implications of declining mail volumes extend beyond financial considerations. As fewer letters are sent, the relevance of Canada Post's infrastructure, including sorting facilities and delivery networks, comes under scrutiny. Maintaining a vast network of postal services that was once necessary for a thriving mail system now poses a significant burden. Without a proactive strategy to recalibrate these resources, Canada Post risks becoming a relic of a bygone era, unable to meet the expectations of modern consumers who value speed and convenience.

Moreover, the decline has also affected employee morale and job security within Canada Post. With fewer mail items to process, the workforce faces uncertainty about job stability. This environment can lead to decreased productivity and increased turnover, further complicating the organisation's efforts to modernise. Instead of being able to focus on innovation and customer service, Canada Post finds itself in a reactionary mode, dealing with the fallout of a shrinking market without a clear vision for the future.

In conclusion, the decline in mail volumes presents a multifaceted challenge for Canada Post that encompasses operational inefficiencies, financial strain, and workforce concerns. The management's failure to modernise in the face of these changes has left the Crown Corporation at a crossroads. Without a decisive shift towards embracing digital solutions and rethinking its service offerings, Canada Post risks losing its position as a vital service provider in an increasingly digital world. The path to recovery will require bold leadership and innovative thinking to redefine the role of Canada Post in the 21st century.

Customer Complaints and Service Issues

Customer complaints and service issues have become a pervasive concern for Canada Post, illustrating a significant failure in management that has hindered the Crown Corporation's ability to modernise effectively. Over the years, numerous reports have surfaced detailing delayed deliveries, lost packages, and inadequate customer service responses. These issues not only frustrate customers but also undermine the public's trust in an institution that is meant to represent reliability and efficiency in postal services. As the digital age evolves, the expectations for timely and accurate service have increased, yet Canada Post has struggled to meet these demands.

One major factor contributing to the rise in customer complaints is the outdated infrastructure that Canada Post continues to operate. Many of the facilities and systems in use today were designed for a different era, leading to inefficiencies in processing and delivering mail. The lack of investment in modern technology has resulted in bottlenecks that delay service and exacerbate customer dissatisfaction. In contrast, private delivery services have embraced technological advancements, providing real-time tracking and prompt customer support, thus leaving Canada Post at a competitive disadvantage.

Furthermore, the training and support provided to Canada Post employees have not kept pace with the changing landscape of postal services. Employees often find themselves ill-equipped to handle customer inquiries or resolve service issues effectively. This lack of adequate training not only affects employee morale but also leads to inconsistent service quality. Customers frequently report having to navigate a cumbersome process to voice their complaints, often resulting in unresolved issues and a sense of frustration that reflects poorly on the organisation as a whole.

The failure to address customer complaints in a timely and effective manner has significant repercussions for Canada Post's reputation. As social media and online review platforms become more prevalent, negative experiences can amplify quickly, damaging public perception. Customers expect a responsive and adaptive service, yet Canada Post's slow reaction to feedback has created an impression of complacency. This disconnect between customer expectations and service delivery has contributed to a growing perception that Canada Post is out of touch with the needs of the communities it serves.

In conclusion, the ongoing customer complaints and service issues at Canada Post highlight a broader management failure in modernising the Crown Corporation. The inability to adapt to changing consumer expectations, coupled with outdated systems and insufficient employee training, has led to an erosion of trust and satisfaction among the public. For Canada Post to regain its standing as a reliable service provider, it must prioritise addressing these service issues, embracing modern technology, and fostering a customer-centric culture that values feedback and responsiveness. Only then can it hope to bridge the gap between its operational shortcomings and the needs of its clientele.

Failure to Adapt to Digital Trends

The failure to adapt to digital trends has profoundly impacted Canada Post's ability to serve its customers effectively. As the world transitioned into the digital age, with increasing reliance on online communication and e-commerce, Canada Post lagged in integrating digital solutions into its operations. While competitors embraced technological advancements, Canada Post remained anchored in traditional practices, which ultimately hindered its capacity to meet evolving consumer expectations. This resistance to change not only diminished customer satisfaction but also threatened the corporation's relevance in a rapidly transforming marketplace.

One of the primary areas where Canada Post fell short was in its online presence and service offerings. As more businesses and individuals turned to e-commerce, the demand for reliable package delivery services surged. However, Canada Post struggled to streamline its logistics and digital interfaces, resulting in longer delivery times and cumbersome tracking systems. Competitors who adopted user-friendly platforms and efficient logistics gained market share while Canada Post's outdated systems alienated potential customers. This failure to modernise its digital infrastructure created a perception of inefficiency and unreliability.

Paradoxically, Canada Post's management underestimated the importance of digital marketing and customer engagement. In an era where social media and online communication play pivotal roles in consumer decision-making, Canada Post's lack of a robust digital marketing strategy limited its ability to connect with younger demographics. By neglecting to foster a strong online community and engage with customers through digital channels, the corporation missed opportunities to build brand loyalty and attract new users. This oversight reflected a broader reluctance to embrace digital transformation within the organisation.

The impact of this failure to adapt extended beyond customer relations; it also affected Canada Post's internal operations. The shift to digital processes can enhance efficiency, reduce operational costs, and streamline workflows. However, Canada Post's management did not sufficiently invest in training employees or upgrading technology to facilitate this transition. As a result, employees remained reliant on outdated systems and processes, leading to frustration and decreased productivity. The lack of a digital-first mindset within the organisation ultimately stifled innovation and hindered the ability to respond to market demands.

To put it bluntly, Canada Post's failure to adapt to digital trends has had far-reaching consequences for the organisation. The inability to modernise its service offerings and embrace digital marketing strategies has resulted in lost customers and diminished relevance in an increasingly competitive landscape. Additionally, the internal resistance to change has stunted the potential for operational improvements and innovation.

Chapter 4: The Impact of E-Commerce

Rise of Online Shopping

The rise of online shopping has transformed the retail landscape in Canada, fundamentally altering consumer behavior and expectations. With the advent of the internet and the proliferation of smartphones, consumers have become accustomed to the convenience of purchasing goods from the comfort of their homes. This shift began in the late 1990s and has accelerated dramatically over the past two decades, fueled by advancements in technology and changes in consumer preferences. As a result, traditional brick-and-mortar retailers have had to adapt or risk becoming obsolete, leading to a significant increase in the volume of parcels that require efficient delivery systems.

Canada Post, as the national postal service, found itself at a crossroads during this digital revolution. Initially, the organisation saw an increase in parcel delivery due to the rise of e-commerce. However, Canada Post management failed to fully embrace the changes in the market and did not modernise its operations to meet the growing demand for efficient and rapid delivery services. This stagnation can be attributed to a lack of strategic vision and an inability to invest in technology that could have streamlined processes and improved customer service.

Competitors in the logistics and delivery sector began to emerge, offering innovative solutions that catered to the needs of online shoppers. Companies such as Amazon not only provided fast delivery options but also implemented sophisticated logistics networks that enabled them to fulfill orders with remarkable efficiency. In contrast, Canada Post continued to rely on outdated systems and processes, which hindered its ability to compete effectively in the evolving marketplace. This failure to innovate and adapt left many consumers dissatisfied with Canada Post's services, leading them to seek alternatives.

Furthermore, the management of Canada Post struggled to understand the changing dynamics of consumer expectations. As more Canadians turned to online shopping, they began to expect faster shipping times and greater flexibility in delivery options. Canada Post's inability to offer same-day or next-day delivery in many areas became a significant disadvantage. By not investing in the necessary infrastructure and technology, Canada Post alienated a growing segment of the population that prioritised speed and convenience, ultimately jeopardising its relevance in the retail ecosystem.

The rise of online shopping has thus served as a warning about the importance of adaptability in a rapidly changing environment. The failure of Canada Post management to modernise the Crown Corporation has not only impacted its operational efficiency but has also led to a loss of public trust. As the landscape continues to evolve, it is crucial for organisations like Canada Post to learn from these missteps and prioritise innovation to meet the needs of a digitally savvy consumer base. The lessons learned from this experience could serve as a foundation for future growth and relevance in an increasingly competitive market.

Competition from Private Couriers

The rise of private courier services has significantly altered the landscape of mail and package delivery in Canada, posing a formidable challenge to Canada Post. As private companies like FedEx, UPS, and a host of smaller regional couriers expanded their operations, they capitalised on technological advancements and changing consumer preferences. These private couriers often offer faster delivery options, flexible pricing, and improved tracking systems, which have made them increasingly appealing to both businesses and individuals. This shift in consumer behavior has highlighted Canada Post's struggles to adapt to the evolving market demands.

Canada Post's traditional model, primarily focused on letter mail, began to falter as the volume of mail decreased. The advent of digital communication reduced the reliance on postal services, while the boom in e-commerce increased demand for parcel delivery. Private couriers swiftly recognised this shift and tailored their services to cater to the growing number of online shoppers. Their agile business practices allowed them to introduce innovative solutions such as same-day delivery and customisable shipping options, which further entrenched their competitive advantage.

In contrast, Canada Post's management has been criticised for its slow response to these changes. Despite having the infrastructure and resources to compete effectively, the organisation has struggled with bureaucratic inertia and an outdated operational model. Efforts to modernise have often been piecemeal and reactive rather than proactive, leading to missed opportunities in a rapidly changing market. This lack of agility has resulted in a diminishing market share and consumer confidence as customers increasingly turn to private couriers for their delivery needs.

Moreover, the regulatory framework surrounding Canada Post has further complicated its ability to compete. As a Crown corporation, Canada Post is subject to specific mandates and constraints that do not apply to private couriers. These regulations can hinder its ability to adjust pricing structures or implement innovative service offerings quickly. In contrast, private companies are free to pivot and adapt their business models without the same level of oversight, allowing them to seize market opportunities more effectively.

The competition from private couriers underscores the pressing need for Canada Post to reevaluate its strategic direction and embrace a more modernised approach to service delivery. To regain its footing in the market, Canada Post must leverage its existing strengths while addressing its weaknesses. This involves not only adopting new technologies and service models but also fostering a culture of innovation within its management structure. The challenge ahead is significant, but with decisive action, Canada Post can still reclaim its relevance in the evolving landscape of postal services.

Missed Opportunities in E-Commerce Delivery

Missed opportunities in e-commerce delivery have significantly impacted the effectiveness of Canada Post as a key player in the modern logistics landscape. The rise of e-commerce has transformed consumer expectations, demanding faster and more reliable delivery services. However, Canada Post has struggled to adapt its operations to meet these evolving needs. This failure not only reflects a lack of strategic foresight but also reveals a deeper systemic issue within the management of the Crown Corporation.

One of the most notable missed opportunities was the failure to invest in technology and infrastructure that support efficient last-mile delivery. As online shopping surged, competitors began to leverage advanced logistics technologies, such as real-time tracking and automated sorting systems. Canada Post, however, remained reliant on outdated processes that hindered its ability to compete. The inability to modernise delivery systems not only resulted in slower service but also diminished customer satisfaction, leading to a decline in market share.

In the world of the current market business idea of "survival of the fittest" we loathfully insinuate that the management of the company missed the boat. Canada Post overlooked the importance of partnerships that could enhance its delivery network. In a rapidly evolving e-commerce landscape, collaboration with private logistics companies and local delivery startups could have expanded Canada Post's reach and improved service options. By failing to establish these strategic alliances, the corporation missed a critical opportunity to adapt its services to the needs of smaller retailers and individual sellers who rely on efficient shipping solutions to compete in the marketplace.

Additionally, Canada Post's management failed to recognise the significance of customer feedback in shaping delivery services. As e-commerce consumers increasingly prioritise convenience and flexibility, Canada Post had the chance to innovate its offerings based on user preferences. However, the lack of a robust feedback mechanism prevented the corporation from understanding and addressing customer pain points, such as delivery times, package tracking, and service reliability. This disconnect not only alienated existing customers but also deterred potential clients who might have preferred Canada Post's services over those of competitors.

Lastly, the overall management approach at Canada Post did not adequately embrace a culture of innovation. In an era where agility and responsiveness are crucial, the organisation remained slow to implement changes that could enhance its service delivery. The reluctance to experiment with new business models, such as subscription-based services or enhanced parcel locker systems, resulted in missed chances to engage with a broader customer base. As e-commerce continues to grow, the failure to seize these opportunities highlights a critical need for Canada Post to rethink its strategies and embrace a more dynamic approach to service delivery.

Chapter 5: Communication Breakdown

Internal Communication Failures

Internal communication failures at Canada Post have significantly contributed to the organisation's inability to modernise effectively. These failures manifest in various ways, including unclear messaging, lack of transparency, and inadequate feedback mechanisms. When employees do not understand the goals and strategies of management, their ability to contribute meaningfully to modernisation efforts is severely compromised. This gap in understanding can create an environment of confusion and frustration, ultimately hindering progress.

One of the primary issues in internal communication at Canada Post has been the inconsistency in messaging from management. Leadership often failed to provide coherent updates regarding strategic initiatives, leading to a disconnect between frontline employees and management objectives. Employees reported feeling uninformed about the direction of the company, which fostered skepticism about management's commitment to modernisation. When messages are unclear or contradictory, it becomes challenging for employees to align their efforts with the organisation's modernisation goals.

Transparency has also been a significant concern. Canada Post has struggled to foster an open dialogue between management and employees, which is essential for building trust and collaboration. Without transparent communication, employees may feel excluded from decision-making processes, leading to a lack of ownership over their work. This exclusion can stifle innovative ideas that could drive modernisation, as employees may hesitate to share their suggestions or concerns when they feel their voices are not valued.

Furthermore, the absence of effective feedback mechanisms has hindered the internal communication process. Employees need to have avenues to express their thoughts and concerns, especially when it comes to changes in processes and technology. Without these channels, management misses critical insights that could inform their strategies. Feedback loops are essential for continuous improvement and adaptation, and the neglect of this aspect has left Canada Post lagging in its modernisation efforts.

Ultimately, the internal communication failures at Canada Post have created a significant barrier to modernisation. To overcome these challenges, the organisation must prioritise clear, consistent messaging, foster transparency, and establish robust feedback mechanisms. By addressing these issues, Canada Post can cultivate a more engaged workforce that is better equipped to contribute to the company's modernisation initiatives, ultimately positioning itself for success in a rapidly changing postal landscape.

External Stakeholder Engagement

External stakeholder engagement is a critical component of any organisation's strategy, particularly for a Crown corporation like Canada Post. Engaging with stakeholders such as consumers, businesses, community organisations, and government entities is essential for understanding their needs, expectations, and concerns. Canada Post's failure to effectively engage these external stakeholders has contributed to its inability to modernise and adapt to the rapidly changing postal landscape. By neglecting to foster meaningful relationships and open lines of communication, Canada Post has missed opportunities to align its services with the evolving demands of the public and the marketplace.

One of the primary stakeholders in Canada Post's operations is the general public, which relies on postal services for personal and business communication. Over the years, there has been a discernible shift in how people communicate and transact, primarily driven by technology. Canada Post's management has not adequately acknowledged or responded to this shift, leading to a disconnect between the corporation's offerings and the expectations of the public. For instance, many consumers now prefer digital communication methods over traditional mail, yet Canada Post has been slow to innovate its services to include more digital solutions. This lack of engagement with public sentiment has hindered the corporation's ability to modernise effectively.

Businesses also represent a significant external stakeholder group that Canada Post must consider. The growth of e-commerce has transformed the landscape of shipping and delivery services, and businesses are increasingly looking for efficient, reliable, and cost-effective solutions. However, Canada Post's management has not taken sufficient steps to engage with the business sector to understand their needs fully. As a result, businesses have sought alternatives that provide the speed and flexibility they require, ultimately undermining Canada Post's market position. The failure to capture this vital feedback loop has stifled innovation and adaptation within the organisation.

Community organizations and local governments also play a crucial role in shaping the landscape in which Canada Post operates. These entities often have insights into the specific needs and challenges faced by their communities. Canada Post's management has historically overlooked these voices, resulting in missed opportunities to tailor services to better serve local populations. For example, feedback from community organisations could have informed the development of services that address rural and remote areas' unique challenges, thus expanding Canada Post's reach and relevance. This disengagement has not only affected service delivery but has also eroded trust and support among key community stakeholders.

The government, as the owner of Canada Post, holds significant influence over its operations and strategic direction. Effective engagement with government stakeholders is essential for securing necessary investments and policy support for modernisation efforts. Canada Post's management has struggled to present a compelling case for modernisation, often failing to articulate how proposed changes align with national interests and the broader goals of public service. This disconnect has resulted in a lack of proactive support and funding from the government, further stalling the corporation's modernisation initiatives. Engaging external stakeholders effectively is not merely a best practice; it is essential for Canada Post to navigate the complexities of the postal industry and ensure its future viability.

Public Perception and Trust Issues

Public perception of Canada Post has been significantly influenced by its management decisions over the years, particularly regarding modernisation efforts. Many Canadians view the organisation as lagging behind in adapting to the rapid changes in the postal and logistics industry. This perception is not only shaped by the visible inefficiencies in service delivery but also by the lack of innovative solutions that align with the expectations of a tech-savvy populace. The disconnect between public needs and the services offered contributes to a growing skepticism about the organisation's ability to evolve in a competitive landscape.

Trust issues have arisen as Canada Post has struggled to keep pace with private sector competitors who have embraced technology and customer-centric approaches. Consumers have increasingly turned to alternative delivery services that promise faster, more reliable, and more transparent options. This shift has left Canada Post in a precarious position, where its traditional image of reliability is undermined by service delays and operational challenges, further eroding public confidence. The failure to communicate effectively about the steps being taken to modernise and improve services has compounded these trust issues.

The management of Canada Post has often been criticised for its reactive rather than proactive strategies. Instead of anticipating the changing needs of consumers, the organisation has tended to implement changes only after facing significant public backlash or competitive pressure. This approach has resulted in a perception that Canada Post is out of touch with its customer base, leading to frustration among users who expect timely and efficient services. The inability to clearly articulate a vision for modernisation has left many Canadians questioning the commitment of management to address these challenges.

In addition to operational inefficiencies, public trust has been further compromised by instances of miscommunication and lack of transparency.

When consumers encounter issues such as lost packages or prolonged delivery times, they often find it difficult to obtain clear answers or satisfactory resolutions. This lack of responsiveness not only frustrates customers but also fosters a sense of distrust toward the organisation. As Canada Post navigates this complex landscape, it must prioritise building stronger communication channels that reassure the public of its dedication to improvement and accountability.

To rebuild public trust, Canada Post must undertake a concerted effort to engage with its customers and demonstrate a commitment to modernization. This involves not only investing in technology and infrastructure but also fostering a culture of transparency and responsiveness. By actively seeking feedback from the public and addressing their concerns, Canada Post can begin to bridge the gap between its operations and the expectations of its customers. A renewed focus on customer service and modernisation will be crucial in reshaping public perception and restoring trust in this vital Crown Corporation.

Chapter 6: Technology and Innovation

Resistance to Technological Change

Resistance to technological change within Canada Post has been a significant barrier to the modernisation of the Crown Corporation. This resistance can be attributed to a combination of factors, including organisational culture, fear of job displacement, and an underestimation of the urgency required to adapt to evolving market conditions. The deeply entrenched practices and mindsets within Canada Post have often hindered the adoption of innovative solutions that could enhance operational efficiency and customer service.

One of the key elements contributing to this resistance is the organisational culture prevalent within Canada Post. A traditional mindset has dominated leadership and employee attitudes, leading to a reluctance to embrace new technologies. This culture often prioritises maintaining existing processes over exploring potential improvements. Employees, accustomed to established routines, tend to view technological changes as threats rather than opportunities. As a result, initiatives aimed at modernisation have faced pushback from within the organisation itself, impeding progress.

Fear of job displacement further exacerbates resistance to technological change. Employees may perceive automation and digital solutions as a direct threat to their roles, leading to anxiety and opposition. This fear is not unfounded, as the introduction of new technologies can indeed alter job descriptions and eliminate certain tasks. However, the failure to communicate the potential benefits of these changes, such as the creation of new roles and the enhancement of existing ones, has left many workers feeling vulnerable and resistant. This dynamic has created a culture of defensiveness rather than one that fosters collaboration and innovation.

The urgency of modernisation has often been underestimated by Canada Post management. With the rapid evolution of the postal and logistics industries, driven by advancements in technology and changing consumer expectations,

Canada Post has lagged behind competitors. While other organisations have successfully integrated technology to improve service delivery and operational effectiveness, Canada Post's slow response reflects a broader reluctance to change. This inertia has not only hindered its ability to compete but has also alienated customers who increasingly expect more efficient, technology-driven services.

To overcome resistance to technological change, Canada Post must foster a culture that values innovation and adaptability. This requires leadership to actively engage with employees, addressing their concerns and highlighting the long-term benefits of modernisation. By investing in training programs and providing clear communication about the positive impacts of new technologies, Canada Post can begin to shift the perception of change from a threat to an opportunity. Embracing a proactive approach to technological advancement will be essential for Canada Post to remain relevant and competitive in an increasingly digital landscape.

Investment in Modern Solutions

Investment in modern solutions is crucial for any organisation aiming to stay relevant and competitive in an ever-evolving marketplace. For Canada Post, a Crown Corporation with a storied history, the failure to adequately invest in modern technologies and processes has had far-reaching consequences. The post office, once an essential service provider, has faced significant challenges in adapting to the digital age, leading to a decline in service quality and customer satisfaction. This subchapter will explore the implications of these missed opportunities and the pressing need for Canada Post to embrace modern solutions.

The advent of digital communication has transformed how people interact and conduct business. With the rise of email, social media, and other online platforms, traditional mail services have seen a dramatic decline. Canada Post's management underestimated this shift, leading to a lack of strategic investments in technology that could have enhanced efficiency and customer engagement. Instead of developing robust digital services that could complement their traditional offerings, the organisation remained largely focused on its legacy systems, which hampered its ability to innovate and respond to changing consumer expectations.

Moreover, the lack of investment in modern logistics and delivery systems has further compounded Canada Post's challenges. Competitors have leveraged technology to streamline operations, reduce delivery times, and improve tracking capabilities. Canada Post lagged in adopting these advancements, resulting in a diminished service experience for customers. The absence of an integrated approach that combines physical and digital services has left Canada Post vulnerable to competition from private sector alternatives that offer more flexible and user-friendly options.

The consequences of failing to invest in modern solutions extend beyond operational inefficiencies; they also impact the overall perception of Canada Post as a reliable service provider. Public trust is essential for any organisation, and Canada Post's inability to modernise has eroded confidence among its customer base. As consumers increasingly seek convenient and efficient services, the perception of Canada Post as outdated has contributed to a loss of market share. The organisation must recognise that investing in modernisation is not merely a financial decision but a critical step in rebuilding its reputation and restoring public confidence.

The failure of Canada Post management to invest in modern solutions has had significant repercussions for the Crown Corporation. As the landscape of communication and logistics continues to evolve, it is imperative for Canada Post to reassess its strategies and embrace the opportunities that modern technology presents. By prioritising investment in innovative solutions, Canada Post can revitalise its services, enhance customer satisfaction, and ultimately secure its place as a leading service provider in the digital era. The path forward lies in recognising the necessity for change and committing to the investments that will enable Canada Post to thrive in a competitive marketplace.

The Importance of Innovation Culture

Innovation culture plays a critical role in the success and adaptability of organisations, particularly in the context of a Crown Corporation like Canada Post. In an era marked by rapid technological advancement and shifting consumer expectations, fostering a culture that embraces innovation is essential. Such a culture empowers employees to think creatively, experiment with new ideas, and adapt to changing market dynamics. Unfortunately, Canada Post management has often fallen short in cultivating this environment, resulting in missed opportunities to modernise and enhance operational efficiency.

A strong innovation culture encourages collaboration across all levels of an organisation. When employees feel supported in sharing their ideas, they are more likely to contribute to the development of innovative solutions. This collaborative spirit can lead to the identification of processes that require improvement, ultimately driving the organisation forward. Canada Post has historically operated in silos, which has hindered communication and collaboration. This lack of interconnectedness has stifled creative thinking and limited the organisation's ability to respond effectively to the challenges posed by digital transformation.

Moreover, an innovation culture requires leadership that champions change and encourages risk-taking. Leaders must create an environment where employees feel safe to propose bold ideas without the fear of failure. In contrast, Canada Post management has often prioritised risk aversion, focusing on maintaining the status quo rather than exploring new opportunities. This approach has led to stagnation, as the organisation has struggled to keep pace with competitors who are willing to embrace change and invest in innovative technologies and services.

Employee engagement is another vital component of an effective innovation culture. When workers are actively engaged in the innovation process, they are more likely to take ownership of their contributions and feel aligned with the organisation's goals. Canada Post has faced challenges in engaging its workforce, as many employees have felt disconnected from the decision-making processes that impact their roles. This disconnect can dampen morale and diminish the motivation to pursue innovative initiatives, further exacerbating the organisation's struggle to modernise.

In conclusion, the failure to establish a robust innovation culture has significantly contributed to Canada Post's inability to adapt to the evolving postal landscape. By neglecting the importance of collaboration, leadership support, and employee engagement, the management has missed critical opportunities to innovate and modernise its services. For Canada Post to thrive in the future, it must prioritise the development of an innovation culture that fosters creativity, embraces change, and empowers its workforce to contribute to the organisation's ongoing evolution.

Chapter 7: Employee Relations and Morale

Labor Relations History

Labor relations history at Canada Post is marked by a series of complex interactions between management and employee unions, reflecting broader trends in labor movements across Canada. The roots of these relationships can be traced back to the establishment of the postal service as a Crown corporation in 1867. Initially, labor relations were characterised by a lack of formal union representation, with workers often subject to arbitrary management decisions. Over time, as the labor movement gained momentum in Canada, postal workers began to organise themselves, leading to the formation of unions that sought to negotiate better wages, working conditions, and job security.

The first major breakthrough in labor relations at Canada Post occurred in the late 1960s when the postal workers' union successfully negotiated its first collective bargaining agreement. This marked a significant shift in the dynamics between management and employees, as it established a framework for negotiations and dispute resolution. The agreement provided postal workers with a voice in the workplace and laid the groundwork for future negotiations. However, the relationship between labor and management remained contentious, with periodic strikes and disputes highlighting the ongoing tensions.

Throughout the 1970s and 1980s, labor relations at Canada Post were further complicated by economic challenges and changing political landscapes. The introduction of automation and modernisation initiatives led to fears of job losses among workers. In response, unions became more militant, advocating not only for job security but also for fair compensation in the face of increasing workloads and technological advancements. Strikes became a common occurrence during this period, as workers sought to assert their rights and negotiate better terms with management.

The 1990s ushered in a new era of labor relations at Canada Post, with the introduction of significant reforms aimed at modernising the corporation. However, these changes often came at the expense of workers' rights and job security. Management's push for efficiency and cost-cutting measures led to conflicts with unions, as employees resisted changes that they perceived as detrimental to their livelihoods. The struggle for a balance between modernisation and fair labor practices became a defining feature of the decade, setting the stage for ongoing disputes in the years to come.

In the 21st century, Canada Post has continued to grapple with the challenges of labor relations amid rapid technological advancements and shifts in consumer behavior. The failure to adequately modernise while addressing employee concerns has led to a persistent sense of dissatisfaction among workers. The history of labour relations at Canada Post highlights the need for a more collaborative approach between management and unions, emphasising the importance of addressing workers' needs while navigating the complexities of modernisation. As Canada Post moves forward, understanding this historical context is essential for developing effective strategies that prioritise both efficiency and employee well-being.

Impact of Management Decisions on Employees

Management decisions play a pivotal role in shaping the workplace environment and influencing employee morale, productivity, and overall job satisfaction. At Canada Post, the management's failure to modernise the Crown Corporation has had a profound impact on employees. The decisions made at the upper echelons of the organisation have often overlooked the needs and aspirations of the workforce, leading to a disconnection between management and employees. This disconnect has fostered an atmosphere of frustration and disengagement, where employees feel undervalued and unheard.

One of the most significant impacts of management decisions has been the lack of investment in technology and infrastructure. As the postal service landscape evolved with the rise of digital communication and e-commerce, Canada Post management remained stagnant in its approach. Employees found themselves struggling with outdated systems and processes, which hindered their ability to perform efficiently. This not only affected their job performance but also diminished their enthusiasm for the work they were doing, leading to a decline in overall morale.

Furthermore, the management's approach to communication has contributed to a culture of silence and uncertainty among employees. When decisions regarding changes in operations, job roles, and organisational structure are made without consulting or informing staff, it creates an environment of mistrust. Employees at Canada Post have expressed concerns about feeling left in the dark regarding their future and the direction of the company. This lack of transparency can lead to increased anxiety and resentment, ultimately affecting productivity and employee retention.

The failure to address employee needs through management decisions has also resulted in a decline in innovation within the organization. A workforce that feels undervalued and ignored is less likely to contribute ideas or engage in creative problem-solving. In a rapidly changing industry, the ability to innovate is crucial for survival, yet management at Canada Post has not fostered an environment that encourages such contributions from its employees. As a result, the organisation risks falling further behind competitors who prioritise employee engagement and harness the potential of their workforce.

Lastly, the impact of management decisions extends beyond immediate job satisfaction and productivity. The long-term consequences of neglecting employee well-being can lead to high turnover rates and a damaged reputation as an employer. Canada Post's struggle to modernise has not only affected existing employees but has also made it difficult to attract new talent. A company that fails to recognise and adapt to the changing needs of its workforce risks losing its competitive edge in an industry that relies heavily on both customer service and employee commitment. Addressing these issues is essential for Canada Post to move forward and regain its position as a leader in the postal industry.

Case Studies of Employee Experiences

In examining the employee experiences at Canada Post, several case studies illustrate the challenges and shortcomings of management in adapting to modern workplace demands. One notable case involves a group of frontline employees who faced significant operational changes due to the rise of e-commerce. As parcel volumes surged, employees were expected to adapt quickly, yet they reported a lack of training and resources to effectively manage the increased workload. This disconnect between management's expectations and the realities on the ground highlighted a failure to recognise the evolving nature of the postal service and the necessary support that employees required to thrive.

Another case study features employees within the sorting facilities who experienced technological upgrades intended to streamline operations. While management promoted these advancements as beneficial, many employees felt that the implementation was rushed and poorly executed. The lack of comprehensive training programs led to confusion and frustration among staff, ultimately impacting productivity and morale. This situation exemplifies a broader issue within Canada Post management, where the focus on modernisation did not account for the human element, resulting in disengaged employees who were left to navigate new systems without adequate guidance.

A third case involves the experiences of customer service representatives who reported feeling undervalued and overwhelmed by the lack of communication from upper management. Many employees expressed concerns about their workload and the increasing customer demands, particularly during peak seasons. In these instances, management's failure to establish a transparent dialogue with employees led to a culture of fear and uncertainty. This gap in communication not only affected employee satisfaction but also hindered the organisation's overall ability to respond effectively to customer needs, revealing a critical misalignment between management strategies and employee realities.

Additionally, a case study focusing on remote workers during the pandemic showcases the challenges posed by inadequate infrastructure and support systems. Employees who transitioned to remote work faced difficulties related to technology access and connectivity. Many reported feeling isolated and disconnected from their teams, and the absence of a coherent remote work policy further exacerbated these issues. This scenario underscores how Canada Post management struggled to embrace modern work trends, leaving employees without the necessary tools and support to navigate unprecedented changes in the workplace.

Finally, the experiences of employees involved in the unionization efforts illustrate the broader implications of management's approach to employee relations. Many workers felt that their voices were not heard, which fueled a desire to organise for better working conditions. The management's resistance to addressing employee grievances only intensified feelings of frustration and alienation. This case study serves as a poignant reminder of the importance of fostering a collaborative relationship between management and employees, as the failure to do so can lead to significant disruptions in the organisation and ultimately hinder its ability to modernise effectively.

Chapter 8: Financial Implications

Analysis of Financial Performance

The financial performance of Canada Post has been a topic of significant scrutiny, particularly in light of its failure to adapt to the evolving landscape of the postal industry. Over the last decade, the organisation has faced declining revenues, primarily due to a substantial reduction in traditional mail volumes. This trend reflects broader shifts in communication and commerce, where digital alternatives have gained prominence. As a Crown Corporation, Canada Post is expected to operate efficiently while serving the public interest, yet its financial outcomes suggest a disconnect between its operational strategies and market realities.

An analysis of Canada Post's financial statements reveals alarming trends in profitability and cost management. Revenue declines have been compounded by rising operational costs, leading to a downward spiral in net income. The corporation's reliance on outdated business models, coupled with the lack of investment in innovative services, has hindered its ability to generate new revenue streams. Consequently, Canada Post has struggled to maintain a sustainable financial footing, calling into question the effectiveness of its management strategies.

Furthermore, the financial performance of Canada Post must be contextualised within its competitive landscape. Other postal and logistics providers have successfully navigated similar challenges by embracing technology and diversifying service offerings. In contrast, Canada Post's slow response to these changes has led to a loss of market share. The management's failure to recognise and act upon competitive threats has resulted in missed opportunities for growth and adaptation, further exacerbating its financial difficulties.

The implications of Canada Post's financial performance extend beyond mere numbers; they reflect a leadership crisis within the organisation. A lack of clear vision and strategic direction has contributed to misalignment between operational goals and the needs of the public. This disconnect has fueled public dissatisfaction and eroded trust in the corporation. Stakeholders, including employees and customers, have expressed concerns about the long-term viability of Canada Post, which is critical for a service that plays a vital role in Canadian society.

A comprehensive analysis of Canada Post's financial performance underscores the urgent need for transformative change within the organisation. The combination of declining revenues, rising costs, and ineffective management practices has created a precarious situation that threatens the very foundation of this Crown Corporation. To reverse the current trajectory, Canada Post must embrace modernisation and innovation, aligning its operations with the demands of a rapidly changing environment. Failure to do so may jeopardise its future and the essential services it provides to Canadians.

Budgeting and Resource Allocation

Budgeting and resource allocation are crucial components in the effective management of any organisation, particularly for a Crown corporation like Canada Post. The ability to allocate financial and human resources wisely directly impacts the organisation's capacity to meet its goals and adapt to changing market conditions. In the case of Canada Post, mismanagement in these areas has contributed to its struggles in modernising operations and remaining competitive. A detailed examination of budgeting practices reveals how inadequate planning and prioritisation have hindered the organisation's progress.

Historically, Canada Post has faced challenges in establishing a clear and strategic budget that aligns with its long-term objectives. The organisation often operated on a reactive basis, addressing immediate financial concerns rather than investing in innovative solutions and future growth. This short-sighted approach resulted in a lack of funding for essential modernisation initiatives, such as upgrading technology and improving customer service. As competitors embraced digital transformation, Canada Post's inability to allocate resources effectively became increasingly evident, leading to a decline in both service quality and customer satisfaction.

The resource allocation process at Canada Post has been plagued by inefficiencies and bureaucratic hurdles. Decision-making often lacks transparency, making it difficult for managers to prioritise projects that would yield the highest returns on investment. The absence of a clear framework for evaluating the effectiveness of resource allocation further exacerbates the situation, resulting in funds being diverted to less impactful initiatives. This misallocation of resources not only stifles innovation but also undermines employee morale, as staff members become frustrated with the organisation's inability to adapt and evolve.

The impact of ineffective budgeting and resource allocation extends beyond financial performance; it also affects the overall organisational culture. When employees witness poor decision-making and a lack of strategic direction, it can lead to disengagement and reduced productivity. In a rapidly changing environment, where agility and responsiveness are essential, Canada Post's failure to foster a culture that embraces change has been detrimental. Employees are less likely to propose innovative ideas or solutions when they perceive that their efforts will not be supported or funded.

To address these issues, Canada Post must prioritise a comprehensive review of its budgeting and resource allocation processes. This involves developing a strategic plan that includes input from various stakeholders, ensuring that all levels of the organisation are involved in the decision-making process. By adopting a more collaborative approach and leveraging data-driven insights, Canada Post can create a budget that not only addresses immediate needs but also positions the organisation for long-term success. Emphasizing transparency, accountability, and innovation in budgeting practices will be essential for the Crown corporation to regain its footing in an increasingly competitive landscape.

Long-Term Sustainability Concerns

Long-term sustainability concerns regarding Canada Post have become increasingly prominent as the organisation struggles to adapt to a rapidly changing landscape. The rise of digital communication and e-commerce has drastically altered the postal industry's operational framework, rendering traditional mail services less relevant. As consumer preferences shift towards instant digital alternatives, Canada Post faces a pressing challenge to stay relevant while ensuring its long-term viability. The failure to modernise its infrastructure and services not only affects its financial stability but also raises questions about its role in Canadian society moving forward.

One of the pivotal factors in assessing Canada Post's sustainability is its reliance on traditional revenue streams, primarily letter mail. With a continuous decline in volume, driven by the widespread adoption of email and online messaging, Canada Post's financial model has been compromised. This over-dependence on a diminishing service highlights a critical misalignment with current consumer behaviors. In contrast, competitors in logistics and parcel delivery have capitalised on the e-commerce boom, leaving Canada Post struggling to compete in a market that demands agility and innovation.

Furthermore, the organisation's governance structure has often been criticized for its lack of responsiveness to emerging trends. A significant concern is the absence of a proactive strategy to embrace digital transformation. While other postal services globally have successfully implemented technology-driven solutions, Canada Post has lagged behind. This failure to integrate modern technology not only hampers operational efficiency but also alienates a customer base that increasingly expects seamless digital experiences. The lack of foresight in management decisions has contributed to a deterioration of public trust and confidence in the corporation's ability to adapt.

Environmental sustainability is another critical aspect that Canada Post must address to secure its future. As climate change becomes an urgent global issue, there is rising pressure on corporations to reduce their carbon footprints. Canada Post's operational practices, including its vehicle fleet and sorting facilities, require modernisation to align with environmental standards. Inadequate attention to sustainability initiatives not only jeopardises Canada Post's reputation but also poses potential regulatory risks. By failing to prioritise eco-friendly practices, the corporation risks alienating environmentally conscious consumers and stakeholders.

Lastly, the cultural mindset within Canada Post must shift towards embracing a long-term vision that prioritises innovation and adaptability. Cultivating a workforce that is open to change and equipped with the necessary skills to drive modernisation is crucial. This involves investing in training and development programs that foster a culture of continuous improvement. Without a commitment to evolving its operational practices and embracing a customer-centric approach, Canada Post risks becoming increasingly irrelevant in an industry characterised by rapid transformation. Addressing these long-term sustainability concerns is essential for maintaining the corporation's status as a vital service provider in Canada's economy.

Chapter 9: Lessons from Other Countries

Comparative Analysis with Other Postal Services

The examination of Canada Post's management failures cannot be complete without a comparative analysis with other postal services around the world. Countries like Germany, the United States, and Japan have undergone significant modernisation efforts, enabling them to adapt to the demands of the digital age and changing consumer behaviors. This analysis highlights the discrepancies in strategic approaches and operational efficiencies that illuminate Canada Post's stagnation in innovation and service enhancement.

In Germany, Deutsche Post has successfully integrated technology into its operations, offering a variety of digital services alongside traditional postal functions. The introduction of parcel lockers and a sophisticated logistics network has allowed for increased efficiency and customer satisfaction. By embracing e-commerce and enhancing its delivery capabilities, Deutsche Post has positioned itself as a leader in postal services. In contrast, Canada Post has struggled to innovate its offerings, often falling back on outdated practices that do not meet the evolving expectations of Canadian consumers.

The United States Postal Service (USPS) presents another contrasting case, showcasing how a proactive approach can lead to significant improvements in service delivery. USPS has invested in technology to streamline operations, including automated sorting and improved tracking systems, which have greatly enhanced customer experience. Additionally, the USPS has adapted its business model to include services like package delivery and same-day delivery options, catering to the growing e-commerce market. Canada Post's reluctance to modernise its infrastructure and services in a similar manner has resulted in a loss of market share and customer trust.

Japan's postal system, which is operated by Japan Post, provides another illustrative example of how effective management and strategic planning can lead to success. Japan Post has diversified its services, integrating financial services with traditional postal operations. This holistic approach has not only ensured financial viability but also strengthened community ties through reliable service. Canada Post's failure to diversify and adapt its service offerings has hindered its ability to compete effectively in both the domestic and global postal markets.

The comparative analysis reveals that Canada Post's management challenges stem from a lack of forward-thinking strategies and an unwillingness to embrace change. While other postal services have recognised the importance of innovation in maintaining relevance, Canada Post has remained mired in bureaucratic inertia. By examining the successes and failures of international counterparts, it becomes evident that a shift in management philosophy and a commitment to modernisation are critical for Canada Post to regain its standing as a competitive and customer-centered service provider in the evolving postal landscape.

Successful modernisation examples

Successful modernisation efforts in various sectors can provide valuable lessons for organisations like Canada Post, which has struggled with its own modernisation initiatives. One prominent example is the modernisation of the United States Postal Service (USPS). Faced with declining mail volumes and increased competition from private delivery services, USPS undertook a comprehensive plan to modernise its operations. This included the implementation of advanced sorting technology and the adoption of digital services that allowed customers to track packages in real-time. These changes not only improved operational efficiency but also enhanced customer satisfaction, demonstrating that a proactive approach to modernisation can yield significant benefits.

Another noteworthy example comes from the United Kingdom's Royal Mail. Recognising the need to adapt to a changing marketplace, Royal Mail invested heavily in technology and infrastructure. The introduction of automated sorting systems and the expansion of parcel delivery services were pivotal in this transformation. Additionally, Royal Mail embraced e-commerce by developing partnerships with online retailers, thus capturing a growing segment of the market. This strategic pivot not only revitalised the company's revenue streams but also positioned it as a leader in the logistics sector, highlighting the importance of aligning modernisation efforts with market demands.

In the private sector, companies like FedEx and UPS have successfully navigated the challenges of modernisation by leveraging technology and data analytics. FedEx, for instance, has integrated advanced tracking systems that provide customers with real-time updates on their shipments, significantly enhancing the user experience. UPS has focused on optimising its delivery routes through sophisticated algorithms that reduce fuel consumption and improve delivery times. These examples illustrate how embracing technology and innovative practices can lead to operational improvements and better customer service, something that Canada Post could have emulated in its modernisation efforts.

The transportation sector also offers compelling examples of successful modernisation, particularly in the realm of public transit. Cities around the world have adopted smart technology solutions to enhance their transit systems. For instance, cities like Singapore and Barcelona have implemented integrated transport systems that utilise real-time data to improve efficiency and user experience. By adopting similar strategies, Canada Post could have transformed its logistics and delivery systems, making them more responsive to customer needs and reducing operational costs.

Ultimately, the successful modernisation examples from various sectors underscore the importance of adaptability and innovation. Organisations that have thrived in the face of change have done so by prioritising customer needs, investing in technology, and being willing to rethink their business models. For Canada Post, learning from these successful cases could have provided a roadmap for overcoming its management failures and effectively modernising its operations. The lessons from these examples highlight that a commitment to transformation, aligned with strategic vision and customer engagement, is essential for any organisation aiming to succeed in a rapidly evolving landscape.

Applicability to Canada Post

The applicability of the management failures at Canada Post can be observed through various lenses, particularly in the context of its inability to modernise effectively. Over the past decade, Canada Post has faced a myriad of challenges that stem not only from technological advancements but also from shifts in consumer behavior and expectations. The organisation's resistance to embracing new operational models has left it lagging behind private sector competitors, ultimately impacting its service delivery and financial sustainability. This stagnation has raised significant concerns among stakeholders regarding the future viability of the postal service in an increasingly digital world.

One of the critical areas where Canada Post's management has faltered is in the integration of technology into its operations. While other postal services around the world have adopted advanced logistics and tracking systems, Canada Post has been slow to implement similar innovations. The lack of a robust digital strategy has hindered the corporation's ability to offer timely and efficient services, leading to customer dissatisfaction. Furthermore, the failure to harness data analytics for decision-making processes has resulted in missed opportunities to optimise delivery routes, reduce operational costs, and enhance customer engagement.

In addition to technological shortcomings, Canada Post has struggled with adapting its business model to reflect the evolving landscape of communication and commerce. The shift towards e-commerce has transformed the postal service's role in society, yet Canada Post has been hesitant to pivot in response. While competitors have diversified their offerings to include same-day delivery and flexible shipping options, Canada Post has remained entrenched in traditional methods, thereby alienating a customer base that increasingly prioritises speed and convenience. This rigidity has not only affected customer loyalty but has also resulted in a decline in revenue as consumers turn to more agile alternatives.

Moreover, the management of Canada Post has faced criticism for its lack of transparency and accountability. Stakeholders, including employees and the public, have expressed frustration over the decision-making processes that seem disconnected from the realities of the marketplace. The absence of a clear vision for modernisation has led to a culture of complacency, where innovative ideas are stifled, and employee morale suffers. This disconnect not only impacts the internal dynamics of the organisation but also affects how Canada Post is perceived by the public, further eroding trust in its ability to serve as a reliable national service.

Ultimately, the applicability of these failures to Canada Post underscores a broader narrative about the challenges faced by Crown corporations in adapting to modern expectations. The case of Canada Post serves as a cautionary tale about the importance of proactive management in the face of change. For the corporation to regain its footing, it must embrace a comprehensive strategy that prioritises innovation, customer service, and accountability. Only through such a transformation can Canada Post hope to navigate the complexities of the contemporary landscape and fulfill its mandate as a vital service for Canadians.

Chapter 10: Recommendations for the Future

Strategic Planning for Modernisation

Strategic planning for modernisation at Canada Post is an essential topic that reveals the systemic failures within its management framework. In recent years, significant shifts in consumer behavior, technology, and market competition have highlighted the urgent need for Canada Post to evolve. Unfortunately, the organisation's response has been sluggish, leading to missed opportunities and an inability to compete effectively with private carriers and digital alternatives. This subchapter will examine the strategic planning processes—or lack thereof—that have contributed to the ongoing challenges facing Canada Post.

A fundamental aspect of effective strategic planning is the ability to adapt to changing market conditions. Canada Post has struggled with this adaptability, primarily due to an outdated operational model that prioritises traditional mail services over innovative solutions. The failure to recognise and act upon the increasing demand for parcel delivery services, spurred by the rise of e-commerce, has left the organisation vulnerable. Rather than embracing digital transformation and integrating new technologies, Canada Post has often relied on legacy systems that impede operational efficiency and customer satisfaction.

Moreover, strategic planning requires a clear vision and mission that align with evolving consumer needs. Canada Post's leadership has repeatedly failed to articulate a compelling vision for modernisation that resonates with both employees and customers. This lack of direction has not only demotivated staff but has also eroded public confidence in the Crown Corporation. In a rapidly changing landscape, a cohesive strategy that emphasises transparency, accountability, and responsiveness is critical for engaging stakeholders and fostering a culture of innovation.

The role of data analytics in strategic planning cannot be overstated. Canada Post has not sufficiently leveraged data to inform its decision-making processes.

A comprehensive understanding of market trends, customer preferences, and operational performance is essential for crafting effective strategies. By neglecting to utilise data-driven insights, Canada Post has missed opportunities to optimise its service offerings, enhance customer experiences, and improve overall operational effectiveness. This oversight underscores a broader issue of inadequate investment in modern tools and technologies that are essential for competitiveness.

Finally, successful modernisation efforts require collaboration and partnership within the organisation and with external stakeholders. Canada Post has often operated in silos, failing to foster an inclusive culture that encourages cross-functional teamwork and innovation. Engaging with stakeholders, including employees, customers, and industry partners, is vital for identifying challenges and co-creating solutions. A more collaborative approach to strategic planning could enable Canada Post to harness diverse perspectives and expertise, ultimately driving the modernisation agenda forward. As Canada Post navigates the complexities of modernisation, addressing these strategic planning failures will be crucial in ensuring its relevance and success in the future.

Enhancing Customer Service

Enhancing customer service is a critical component in addressing the shortcomings of Canada Post management. The corporation's inability to adapt to modern customer expectations has resulted in a deterioration of public trust and satisfaction. To enhance customer service, Canada Post must prioritise understanding the evolving needs of its diverse customer base. This involves not only evaluating current service offerings but also actively seeking feedback from customers to identify areas for improvement. Implementing regular surveys and focus groups could provide valuable insights that guide the development of services that align more closely with consumer demands.

Investing in technology is another essential step for Canada Post to enhance its customer service. The rise of e-commerce and digital communication has changed how customers interact with postal services. By modernising its IT infrastructure, Canada Post can streamline processes, reduce wait times, and improve the overall efficiency of its services. Integrating automated systems and user-friendly interfaces for online transactions would allow customers to manage their postal needs more conveniently. Furthermore, the adoption of mobile applications could enable customers to track shipments, schedule pickups, and access customer service support more effectively.

Training and developing staff is equally important in the quest to enhance customer service. A well-informed and motivated workforce is crucial for delivering exceptional service. Canada Post should implement comprehensive training programs that emphasise customer engagement, problem-solving skills, and effective communication. Empowering employees to take ownership of customer interactions and resolve issues promptly will not only improve the customer experience but also foster a culture of accountability within the organisation. Regular workshops and performance evaluations can help maintain high service standards and encourage continuous improvement.

Another significant aspect of enhancing customer service is improving communication strategies. Canada Post must ensure that information regarding services, policies, and changes is effectively communicated to all stakeholders. This includes utilising multiple channels such as social media, email newsletters, and traditional advertising to reach a broader audience. Transparent communication builds trust and keeps customers informed, which is essential for maintaining loyalty. Additionally, Canada Post should consider establishing a dedicated customer service hotline that offers real-time assistance, thereby demonstrating a commitment to addressing customer inquiries and concerns promptly.

Finally, fostering a customer-centric culture within Canada Post is vital for long-term success. This involves instilling the belief that customer satisfaction is paramount at every level of the organisation. Leadership must lead by example, prioritising customer service in decision-making processes and recognising employees who excel in delivering exceptional service. By embedding a customer-first mindset into the corporate ethos, Canada Post can create an environment where employees feel empowered to prioritise customer needs. Ultimately, enhancing customer service will not only address the current management failures but also position Canada Post as a forward-thinking and responsive organisation in an increasingly competitive landscape.

Building a Forward-Thinking Culture

Building a forward-thinking culture within an organisation like Canada Post is essential for navigating the complexities of modern business landscapes. A forward-thinking culture is characterised by adaptability, innovation, and a proactive approach to change. Unfortunately, Canada Post has struggled to cultivate such an environment, which has hindered its ability to respond effectively to the evolving needs of the public and the challenges posed by technological advancements. As the world shifts towards digitalisation, it is imperative for organisations to embrace a culture that prioritises innovation and responsiveness.

One of the key elements in fostering a forward-thinking culture is encouraging open communication and collaboration among employees at all levels. At Canada Post, management has often operated in silos, limiting the exchange of ideas and insights that could drive innovation. By breaking down these barriers and promoting a culture of collaboration, Canada Post could harness the collective intelligence of its workforce. This approach not only empowers employees but also creates a sense of ownership and accountability for the organization's direction and success.

Leadership plays a crucial role in shaping organisational culture. In Canada Post's case, there has been a noticeable lack of visionary leadership that inspires and motivates employees to embrace change. Effective leaders should actively champion new ideas and demonstrate a commitment to modernisation. By setting a clear vision for the future and aligning the organisation's goals with that vision, leaders at Canada Post can instill a sense of purpose and urgency among employees, encouraging them to think creatively about solutions to the challenges the organisation faces.

Investing in employee development is another critical aspect of building a forward-thinking culture. Continuous learning and skill enhancement are vital for keeping pace with technological advancements and market demands. Canada Post has historically underinvested in training and development programs, leading to a workforce that may lack the necessary skills to adapt to a rapidly changing environment. By prioritising professional development and providing employees with the tools they need to succeed, Canada Post can foster a culture of innovation and adaptability, ultimately positioning itself for long-term success.

Finally, embracing failure as a learning opportunity is essential for cultivating a forward-thinking culture. In many organisations, including Canada Post, there is often a fear of failure that stifles creativity and experimentation. To truly innovate, employees must feel safe to take risks and explore new ideas without the fear of negative repercussions. By creating an environment that encourages experimentation and views setbacks as valuable learning experiences, Canada Post can inspire its workforce to pursue innovative solutions and remain agile in the face of change. This cultural shift is necessary for the organisation to thrive in an increasingly competitive landscape.

Chapter 11: Conclusion

Summarizing the Management Failures

The management failures at Canada Post have become a significant case study in the realm of public sector administration and corporate governance. As the digital landscape evolved, Canada Post struggled to adapt its traditional mail service model to the changing needs of consumers and businesses. This failure to modernise can be traced back to a series of poor strategic decisions, lack of foresight, and an inability to embrace innovation. The result has been a decline in public trust and a growing sense of frustration among stakeholders who depend on reliable postal services.

One of the primary management failures was the inability to recognise and respond adequately to the rise of digital communication. As email and online messaging became prevalent, Canada Post continued to invest heavily in its traditional mail services without developing a comprehensive strategy for integrating digital solutions. This oversight not only alienated younger generations who prefer electronic communication but also limited the corporation's ability to diversify its revenue streams. Consequently, Canada Post found itself at a crossroads, unable to pivot toward a more sustainable business model.

Another critical issue was the organisational culture within Canada Post, which was resistant to change. This culture was characterised by a hierarchical structure that stifled innovation and discouraged employees from proposing new ideas. Management often dismissed suggestions for modernisation, viewing them as threats to the established order rather than opportunities for growth. This lack of an adaptive mindset contributed to a stagnation of ideas and processes, preventing Canada Post from evolving in an increasingly competitive environment.

Furthermore, Canada Post's management exhibited a reactive rather than proactive approach to challenges. Instead of anticipating market trends and customer preferences, leadership often waited until problems became acute before attempting to address them. This reactive stance led to missed opportunities for partnerships and collaborations that could have bolstered the organisation's relevance in a digital age. As competitors emerged with agile business models, Canada Post's failure to act decisively left it lagging behind in service offerings and customer satisfaction.

Lastly, the communication breakdown between management and frontline employees played a crucial role in the failures experienced by Canada Post. Employees, who have invaluable insights into customer needs and operational inefficiencies, often felt unheard and undervalued. This disconnect not only affected employee morale but also limited the organisation's ability to innovate and adapt. By failing to leverage the knowledge and experience of its workforce, Canada Post's management ultimately undermined its potential to modernise effectively and meet the demands of a rapidly changing postal landscape.

The Path Forward for Canada Post

The path forward for Canada Post requires a comprehensive reassessment of its operational strategies and a commitment to embracing innovation. Historically, Canada Post has relied heavily on its traditional postal services, which have seen a significant decline in demand due to the rise of digital communication and e-commerce. To regain relevance, Canada Post must prioritise the modernisation of its infrastructure, including the adoption of advanced technologies that streamline operations and enhance customer experience. This could involve investing in automation for sorting facilities, implementing data analytics for route optimisation, and enhancing online services to meet the evolving needs of consumers.

In addition to technological advancements, Canada Post must also focus on redefining its service offerings. The corporation has an opportunity to position itself as a logistics leader in the e-commerce sector, which has experienced exponential growth in recent years. By expanding its parcel delivery services and creating partnerships with online retailers, Canada Post can leverage its existing network to capture a larger share of the market. This approach would not only improve financial sustainability but also reinforce the corporation's role as a vital service provider in Canadian communities.

Furthermore, engaging with stakeholders is essential for Canada Post's future success. The corporation must foster open lines of communication with employees, customers, and government entities to ensure that its strategies align with the needs and expectations of the public. By soliciting feedback and addressing concerns, Canada Post can build trust and collaboration, which are crucial for implementing changes effectively. Establishing advisory panels or community forums could facilitate this dialogue, allowing for a more inclusive approach to decision-making.

Sustainability should also be a key pillar in Canada Post's path forward. As societal awareness of environmental issues grows, Canada Post must take proactive steps to reduce its carbon footprint. This could include transitioning to a greener fleet, investing in renewable energy sources for its facilities, and promoting eco-friendly packaging options. By positioning itself as a responsible corporate citizen, Canada Post can enhance its brand image and appeal to environmentally conscious consumers while contributing to Canada's climate goals.

Lastly, fostering a culture of innovation within Canada Post is crucial for long-term success. The organisation must encourage its employees to embrace creativity and think outside traditional frameworks. Training programs focused on digital skills and customer service excellence can empower staff to identify and implement improvements. By creating an environment where innovation is celebrated and rewarded, Canada Post can remain agile in a rapidly changing marketplace and ensure its relevance in the years to come.

Final Thoughts on Public Service and Accountability

Public service and accountability are foundational principles that underpin the operation of Crown corporations like Canada Post. As a public entity, Canada Post bears the responsibility of serving the Canadian populace while adhering to the highest standards of transparency and ethical conduct. The management failures observed at Canada Post over recent years highlight the critical need for these principles to be actively practiced and reinforced. When management fails to prioritise accountability, it not only jeopardises the efficiency of services but also erodes public trust, a vital asset for any public institution.

The lack of modernisation within Canada Post's management reflects a broader issue faced by many public service organisations in adapting to the rapid technological advancements and changing consumer expectations. The failure to embrace innovative solutions and modern operational practices has resulted in significant service delivery gaps. As consumers increasingly rely on digital solutions, Canada Post's inability to evolve has not only hindered its competitiveness but has also limited its capacity to meet the diverse needs of Canadians. This stagnation serves as a cautionary tale about the importance of proactive management and the willingness to adapt in today's fast-paced environment.

Moreover, the accountability mechanisms that should have been in place were insufficient to address the shortcomings of the management team. An effective accountability framework not only includes performance metrics but also involves stakeholder engagement and feedback loops that inform decision-making. In the case of Canada Post, there appears to have been a disconnect between management actions and the feedback from employees and customers. This lack of responsiveness to stakeholder concerns contributed to a culture of complacency, where critical issues went unaddressed, further compounding the organisation's challenges.

Public service organisations must recognise that accountability is not merely a regulatory requirement, but a fundamental aspect of their operational ethos. Building a culture of accountability requires strong leadership, transparent communication, and the willingness to confront uncomfortable truths. For Canada Post, embracing these values could pave the way for a more resilient organisation that not only meets current expectations but is also prepared for future challenges. The lessons learned from the management failures of Canada Post serve as a reminder that public institutions must prioritise accountability and modernisation to maintain their relevance and effectiveness.

In conclusion, the failures observed within Canada Post underscore the vital importance of public service and accountability in the management of Crown corporations. As Canada Post navigates its path forward, it must take these lessons to heart, fostering a culture that values transparency, responsiveness, and innovation. By recommitting to these principles, Canada Post can restore public confidence and emerge as a model for effective public service in the modern age. The journey toward accountability and modernisation is essential not only for the success of Canada Post but also for the continued trust and support of the Canadian public it serves.

A cordial note:

For those employees of Canada Post who have constantly given me bright ideas, opinions and a lot of arguments, I could not have been able to write these few pages without your input. I thank you so profoundly with gratitude.

Reference

Unpublished personal papers
Labour relations papers
Personal involvement with postal services for many years.
Social media and newspapers.
Communication with many former employees.
Personal diaries & records
Industrial & Systems Engineering reports.

Also by DM Ole Kiminta

How the Western Democracies failed the world
Supporting Refugees in their Homelands
Dissuading Global War Mongers:
Dissuading war mongers
La Libération Monétaire en Afrique
Canada Post: Management failure to modernise mail systems
Canada Post management failure to modernise mail systems
Canada Post: Management failure to modernise mail systems

About the Author

DM Ole Kiminta is a Canadian of Maasai heritage. He spent many years working in USA, Britain and in Canada. He is an Industrial engineer, Petroleum engineer and Chemical engineer. Ole Kiminta was educated in USA and United Kingdom. Some of his published research work include Material science, carbon fibres and other composite materials, Polymeric materials, and Particle technology. He currently works for the Canadian government and lives in Toronto Canada with his family.

www.ingramcontent.com/pod-product-compliance
Lightning Source LLC
LaVergne TN
LVHW010454160826
845677LV00012B/2481

* 9 7 9 8 2 3 0 9 7 0 5 6 9 *